The Story of Noah and His Ark

Paintings and Verse by George Conklin

VANTAGE PRESS
New York

FIRST EDITION

All rights reserved, including the right of
reproduction in whole or in part in any form.

Copyright © 1992 by George Conklin

Published by Vantage Press, Inc.
516 West 34th Street, New York, New York 10001

Manufactured in the United States of America
ISBN: 0-533-10013-5

0 9 8 7 6 5 4 3 2 1

Building the Ark

"And then on board take kegs of fresh water,
    and food of all kinds, with fodder and grain,
wheat, rye, corn and barley, placed well in store,
    and all manner of vegetable provisions and more."

Supplies and Fresh Water

And the Lord said to Noah, "See now to your wife,
    and to Shem, Ham and Japheth,
    your sons, and their wives;
let all go on board with their chattels and goods,
    for only you, Noah, find grace in my eyes."

To Anne, my wife and inspiration

Noah

And the Lord said to Noah, "Behold, the world
is filled with violence! With a great flood
I shall destroy all men and creatures
save thee, who findest grace in my eyes."

And to Noah the Lord said, "Build thee an ark,
    fifty cubits wide and three hundred long;
build it well of gopher wood, sturdy and strong,
    with rooms and windows and three stories high.

Shem, Ham and Japheth

And then saith the Lord, "Take two of each kind
of bird and beast, of cattle and fowl,
of reptiles, and of every creeping thing,
a female and a male, only two of each kind.

A Call to All Animals

"Bring them all to the ark: two zebras, two bears,
two tigers, two lions, and kangaroos,
giraffes and elephants, monkeys, and deer;
bring them all on board by twos and twos."

Two of Each Kind

So by twos and twos they all went on board.
    Old Noah's word was his strict command;
he made each twosome keep to its place,
    with very little room they were all closely jammed.

All Brought on Board

It rained and the sea rose steadily
    till the ark went adrift with the rising tide;
a blustering wind rose unabated,
    and the ark soon lost all sight of land.

Adrift

It rained for forty days and nights,
    and with no letup Noah feared
the wrath of heaven. Was the Lord's intent
    a deluge that would never clear?

Deluge

The highest hills all soon were covered,
    and thus for a hundred and fifty days
the waters prevailed; but in the seventh month
    on the seventeeth day a mountain appeared.

A Mountain Appears

Then Noah sent from the ark a raven;
    when it came not back he sent a dove.
On the seventh day the dove came back,
    holding in its beak an olive leaf.

Return of the Dove

Now suddenly Noah's ark was grounded
on the rocky side of Mount Ararat,
but the rains of forty nights and days
had left a sea of haze and fog.

The Ark Goes Aground

Till all at once the sun shone forth
    from east to west and north to south,
and every creature, large or small,
    streamed from the ark by twos and twos,
    spreading the word of Noah's good news.

Noah's Good News

And the Lord said to Noah, "The world be blessed,
of all my creatures I've chosen thee
to build a noble race; go forth
and multiply abundantly."

To Build a Noble Race

Then he said to Noah, "Guard well this good earth
    with its bountiful fruit, its herbs and its flowers,
and learn well its seed time and harvest time;
    be fruitful, go forth and multiply."

Go Forth and Multiply

And the Lord said, "I'll make a covenant with thee—
   here's proof: my rainbow in the sky
will assure no deluge will come again
   if you do your part and SAVE THE EARTH!"

A Covenant to Save the Earth